A Career In Medical Billing and Coding

-

Is It For Me?

Douglas B. Palmer, CCS-P

Copyright © 2012 Douglas B. Palmer, CCS-P

All rights reserved.

ISBN: 1494314606
ISBN-13: 978-1494314606

DEDICATION

This work is dedicated to the late Doron Raviv, who gave me my start over 20 years ago. To Jim Mooney, who gave me a toolbox that is one of a kind. To Valerie, Stacy, and countless others that have given me the opportunity to pass along the legacy that Doron, Jim, and others have imparted to me. And, to those that will follow in carrying on in the industry with passion, integrity, and the pursuit of excellence.

CONTENTS

	Acknowledgments	vii
	Preface	viii
1	Medical Billing And Coding – An Overview	1
2	Training	5
3	Credentials and Certifications	7
4	Professional Environments and Specialties	9
5	Employment Prospects	11
6	FAQ	12
7	Summary	16
8	Resources	17

ACKNOWLEDGMENTS

I would like to express my gratitude to the many people who saw me through this book; to all those who provided support, talked things over, read, wrote, offered comments, allowed me to quote their remarks and assisted in the editing, proofreading and design.

I would like to thank Lee Shimano, Barb Poole, Sam Cox, DPM., Trevor Romans, and Bill Swensen for their invaluable insight and wisdom over the years.

Last and not least: I beg forgiveness of all those who have been with me over the course of the years and whose names I have failed to mention.

PREFACE

The purpose of this work is to offer those interested in a career in the Medical Billing and Coding field an insight on what they may expect before investing a great amount of time, energy, and expense into a career they may not have enough information about to make an informed decision. It is intended to be an introduction to the field in general and perhaps to answer some of the common questions asked by those considering this career field. While it can not answer every question, the book comes with unlimited email questions to the author to further assist those exploring this career path.

This work is not intended or represented to be an instruction manual or teaching guide in the practice of Medical Billing or Medical Coding.

1 MEDICAL BILLING AND CODING AN OVERVIEW

You may have heard about opportunities in Medical Billing and Coding. You may have even considered a career path in this field. You may know the difference, you may not. A great starting point is to offer an explanation of what these two related processes are, how they are similar, and how they differ. The two processes are part of an overall process in the healthcare field known as Revenue Cycle. The two processes represent a significant segment of the Revenue Cycle. Once the two are understood, it will make the concept of Revenue Cycle much clearer.

While Medical Billing and Coding is a term that is rather common, both in conversation as well as a career field. It is important to note that, chronologically, it would be more correct to refer to them together as Medical Coding and Billing. Let us see why that is by describing each.

Medical Coding

Medical Coding is the process of taking documentation of medical services and translating this written information into standardized numerical representations. In other words, taking text and turning the content of that text into numbers. The important word just mentioned is 'standardized'. This is done for a number of reasons including reimbursement, statistical, and other uses. It provides a very efficient means of collecting and communicating data for these purposes.

Medical Coding requires sharp organization, reading and comprehension skills as well as a foundation in Anatomy and Physiology, Medical Terminology, and Legal and Regulatory concerns. The documentation of healthcare services is a critical function in providing accurate records on the health status of patients as well as the treatment related services provided to patients. This documentation is the responsibility of those charged with providing the services to the patient. Once documented, it becomes the role of the medical coder to translate that written documentation into a standard set of codes for use by a number of other stakeholders including those entities responsible for payment, for health agencies that monitor the health of populations, and more.

Medical Coding uses 3 major coding systems to represent the information contained in a patient treatment record. One system represents the conditions or status of the patient. These are called diagnosis codes. The other 2 systems represent the services and supplies utilized in the diagnosis and treatment of patients. These are referred to as procedure codes. The mastery of assigning these code sets based on the documentation of patient encounters with healthcare providers is the foundation of Medical Coding.

It is important to understand why the need exists to take this written information and convert it into a numerical representation. As previously mentioned, this provides standardization and efficiency. Imagine your checking account. At the bottom of your check are 2 important numbers. These are a Routing Number, which identifies the bank where your account is located and your account number indicating the specifics of your holdings within that bank. Now, imagine if you were to say to the electric company, my name is John Smith, my address is 25 Elm Street in Anytown, and I have money on deposit with Mega Bank, please send them a request for this months utility payment. That would be a rather inefficient and cumbersome process, wouldn't it? Additionally, there are often many ways to record the same information. Let us take a condition, such as Hypertension which is a condition of a patient having above normal blood pressure readings over a consistent period of time. This may be written out completely as Hypertension, it may be abbreviated such as HTN, or it may be represented with symbols such as an arrow pointing up followed by the letters BP. Therefore, assigning a standard code that specifically represents the condition allows for accurate, uniform, and efficient communication of health data. The same is true for representing services performed to patients. Let us say that a patient suffers a wound that requires sutures, or stitches. To accurately communicate this service, there are codes that represent the complexity of the suturing, the extent (length) of the suturing, and the location of the suturing of the wound.

The above examples are only two of thousands upon thousands of possible circumstances where the communication of information is standardized and made efficient through the process of medical coding. In addition, there are very detailed and specific guidelines associated with the coding systems that influence what codes are assigned, when they are assigned, and how they are assigned. This is the function of a Medical Coder. Of course, this is a very brief overview of that role.

Medical Billing

Medical Billing is the process of gathering the information of services rendered as represented by the codes assigned in the Medical Coding process, assigning a billable fee to each service, and invoicing the fees for the services to the appropriate responsible party for payment.

Medical Billing, just as Medical Coding, has its own inherent processes that require mastery including organization, accounting, analysis, and follow up skill sets.

Medical Billing requires sharp organization, accounting, and data analysis skills as well as being influenced and guided by Legal and Regulatory concerns.

Once health services have been categorized and all codes assigned in the Medical Coding process, the role of the Medical Biller begins. This role has many facets to it as well. The development of a bill for services requires that a biller understand who is to be billed and any specific requirements or limitations that apply based on the party to be billed. There may be different fees assigned based on the financially responsible party. Therefore, the invoice or "claim" as it is referred to in the healthcare industry will require the assignment of charges based on the "fee schedule" for that particular responsible party. Medicare, Medicaid, Workers Compensation, No-Fault, HMO, Commercial Insurance, Private Insurance, and "Self-Pay" (where the patient is responsible for payment of the bill) may all have different fees for the same particular service. The formatting or content of the billing may have different requirements based on the responsible party. Complete and accurate information is essential when a bill is generated. For example, having the correct responsible party and the correct identifying information for the responsible party to process a claim is the responsibility of the Medical Biller. In addition, knowing each responsible parties requirements can be a complex and voluminous skill set. This may include such things as where to submit claims, time limits for submissions, billing intervals, and more.

Medical Billing is not limited to simply sending out a claim for medical service fees. Once submitted, the claim becomes an entry into the organizations Accounts Receivable, or money due to the organization that has not yet been received. It can not be left to chance or faith that payment will always be forthcoming. There may be no response at all, or there may be a "denial" of payment, or a request for additional information.

Monitoring unpaid billings, receipt and handling of correspondence regarding claims as well as the receipt of payments and the correct application of payments to the correct financial record is a typical responsibility of the Medical Biller.

An important point is appropriate at this point. The descriptions given of the roles of Medical Biller and Medical Coder are broad and general descriptions of the role of each as a general position in a healthcare organization. It is important to note that there can be high degrees of specialization within both roles either by choice of the individual or by job classification and responsibility requirements. There are many different medical specialties – Internal Medicine, Emergency Medicine, Orthopedics, Neurology, Gastroenterology, Psychiatry, just to name a few for Medical Coding purposes. Likewise, there are many different types of reimbursement that often call for specialization or increased proficiency in terms of a Medical Biller such as Medicare, Medicaid, and Workers Compensation for example. In addition, there are professional service environments such as Physicians Offices, Physical Therapy, Dialysis, and more that differ in structure and responsibility from facilities such as Hospitals, Nursing Homes, Rehabilitation Centers, and more. Therefore, merely learning the basics of either Medical Billing or Medical Coding may just be the beginning for an aspiring candidate. The type of organization often presents an additional learning and knowledge requirement for each role.

The information presented thus far is certainly just an overview of the general responsibilities and roles of the Medical Coder and the Medical Biller. Both roles have their particular set of responsibilities and each is complex and vast.

2 TRAINING

Many years ago, I was young and unemployed. I had very little work history and no idea what opportunities were open to me. I did not have a specific target job. Frankly, I just needed a job. I had worked in a supermarket and enjoyed helping people. I identified Customer Service as a skill that I possessed. Aside from being able to work on airplanes, as a result of my military experience, this seemed to be what I could present to a potential employer as a marketable employment skill. After submitting resumes to a number of different classified advertisements under the heading of Customer Service, I was offered an interview with a Medical Billing company. I recall the manager, his name was Louis, holding up a pile of resumes and while waving them around he asked "Why you? Why should I hire YOU? Look at all the people that have applied for this position!". Well, despite thinking to myself that perhaps I was outmatched and knew virtually nothing about Medical Billing. That, if I were him, I might ask the same question. I must have provided an adequate answer as I was offered the job. From that point on, I embarked on several years of "on the job" training. Some training was formal, other training was simply performing assigned tasks and being coached and supervised. I was promoted twice within a year and was well on my way to what would eventually evolve into a career. This particular job, promotions and all, was primarily a Medical Billing position. As I progressed, I became more and more aware of this process called Medical Coding. I seemed to have reached a plateau in my Medical Billing knowledge and advancement and needed a new challenge. So, I began to seek positions where I would get exposure and experience in Medical Coding. I was fortunate that I was able to find a series of these positions that allowed me to grow into both an accomplished Medical Biller and Medical Coder. That was me. A long journey of self motivation and on the job training.

If you perform and internet search for Medical Billing or Medical Coding training individually, you are likely to find that there are very few programs dedicated to one or the other. They are generally presented in a combined course format. There are also many organizations that offer courses in Medical Billing and Coding. Many community colleges have courses that offer either certificate or some type of degree (usually an Associates Degree) in this field. There are also a large number of career training institutions that offer anything from auto repair to computer specialties...massage therapy, medical assisting, surgical technologist, radiology technology, and of course Medical Billing and Coding.

Medical Billing and Coding, as has been presented thus far, is very vast and technical discipline. It does require mastery and knowledge in a number of areas. These include Medical Terminology, Anatomy and Physiology, Accounting, Insurance and Reimbursement, Legal and Regulatory concepts, and of course very detailed and comprehensive knowledge of the coding systems. In addition, there is a level of general computer knowledge that is required along with proficiency in computer applications that are specific to the healthcare field. The curriculum of a Medical Billing and Coding Course should comprehensively prepare a student in each of these areas. It is important to note that there is a distinct difference between learning the technical theory in a classroom environment and the practical real world application of performing this work in an actual healthcare setting. Many courses offer, or even require, some type of follow on externship to gain practical experience. It is extremely important to emphasize that this is a very involved field with vast amounts of knowledge required and continuous learning required, even amongst industry veterans. Any experienced professional in this field will agree that a state of constant learning and development is required to be successful in this field. More on this will be covered in the section dealing with credentials.

To summarize, there are different options or paths to take to gain training in this field. One can secure an entry level position within a healthcare office or organization and learn while they work. Similarly, one can choose to take a course and develop the theory and technical foundation and then gain practical experience subsequent to that learning path. One is not more correct when compared to the other. The structured course curriculums certainly provide a structured and defined learning experience on a prescribed time line. The on the job learning path can be somewhat less predictable in terms of time and specific content, however it is often just as effective since it is presumably a full time learning experience in the real world.

3 CREDENTIALS AND CERTIFICATIONS

You may have been to a type of medical provider and noticed that there are different credentials a medical professional may possess. Certainly, the most familiar is likely that of an M.D. or Medical Doctor. There are many others such as D.O, DPM, PHD, PA, CNP, NP, DMD, OD, and more. Similarly, there are a number of different credentials that those in the field of Medical Billing and Coding can achieve.

For Medical Coders, there are two nationally recognized and highly respected organizations that grant credentials in Medical Coding and in Health Information Management disciplines. These organizations are : The American Academy of Professional Coders (AAPC) and The American Health Information Management Association (AHIMA). Both organizations are highly regarded for their dedication to setting and maintaining standards of professional knowledge and competency, ethics, and the advancement of the profession. A credential earned from either of these organizations demonstrates a professional level of expertise in the category of the credential earned and is respected nationally by the industry. There is a level of prestige associated with the holding of a credential from one of these organizations. There is also a level of responsibility that is expected and required to maintain these credentials. Each credential requires a certain level of continuing education each year to maintain the credential in good standing. In addition to the prestige and national recognition that earning a credential form either AAPC or AHIMA carries with it, there is a an average of 10% - 15% difference in average salary per year between certified and non-certified coders. While there are certainly positions for coders without a certification, many healthcare organizations require certifications for certain positions. On October 1, 2014 there will be a transition from one diagnosis coding system to another. This is one of the biggest changes in the history of the industry. It will create a work demand that is forecasted to exceed qualified professionals available. By the law of supply and demand, this will significantly increase compensation, particularly among those holding a certification.

For Medical Billers, there are not quite the same level of certifications that would be equal to the AAPC or AHIMA credentials. Certainly not in terms of any particular organizations with the time and standing in the industry when compared to these two organizations. However, there are professional organizations that are highly respected and offer some type of certificate of expertise or competency. Some of these organizations are : Healthcare Financial Management Association (HFMA), Medical Group Management Association (MGMA), National Healthcareer Association (NHA), Healthcare Billing and Management Association (HBMA), and others. In addition, AAPC does have a credential specifically for Medical Billing. The Centers for Medicare and Medicaid Services has also developed certificates for specializing in the billing to these government programs.

There is a distinct difference between Medical Coders and Medical Billers in terms of the types of credentials that can be earned. However, there is little difference in terms of the level of knowledge and expertise that each must possess to be competent and successful.

A final note on certifications and coding certifications in particular. Any of the coding certification exams offered by AAPC or AHIMA are designed to test the individual on their professional competency and knowledge. They are granted as testimonial to a very high level of expertise in the particular area they are granted in. They are in no way easy examinations and in fact, they are by design quite difficult. Much in the same way a layer must pass the Bar Exam or an accountant must pass the CPA. The pass rate has historically been approximately 50% for first time examinees. This is the mission of these organizations and the cornerstone of their highly respected reputations. That is, to provide a benchmark of professional knowledge that employers and industry professionals can rely on with confidence and consistency. It should be emphasized that one must truly master the discipline of Medical Coding to achieve the trusted and esteemed approval and confirmation from these organizations. In summary, it requires dedication to the field and embodiment of its substance to truly earn the mark of a professional.

4 PROFESSIONAL ENVIRONMENTS AND SPECIALTIES

One question that many exploring the field of Medical Billing and Coding often ask is "Where will I be able to find a job?" The Healthcare Industry is the fourth largest industry in the nation behind Real Estate, Government (which is incidentally the largest payer of healthcare services in the country), and Finance and Insurance (note – insurance which would include the significant health insurance industry) so it stands to reason that there is plenty of opportunity. Every healthcare provider which includes Medical Offices of all specialties, other outpatient services such as Radiology Canters (X-Ray, CT Scan, MRI, etc), Dialysis Centers, Physical Therapy providers, Hospitals, Nursing Homes, and more need to bill and be paid for the services they provide. There is no shortage of medical providers in this industry.

In general, there are 2 broad categories of healthcare providers :
- Facilities
- Professional Providers

Insert chapter four text here. Insert chapter four text here. Insert chapter Amongst these there are areas where professionals will specialize. For many Medical Billers and Coders, there is an equal need to specialize. Below is an expansion of the 2 categories above to indicate further specialization. It is in no way intended to be complete, but is an example of areas that Medical Billers and Medical Coders further specialize due the nature of the organizations services.

Facilities – Such as Hospitals
- Inpatient Services
- Outpatient Medical Clinic
- Ambulatory Surgery
- Ancillary Services – Lab, Radiology, etc

Professional Providers – Such as Physicians
- Surgeons (Gastroenterology, Orthopedic, Cardiothoracic to name a few for example)
- Oncologists (Chemotherapy)
- Physical Medicine and Rehabilitation
- Pain Management
- Psychiatric Service
- Obstetrics and Gynecology
- Neurology

As you can see, simply having a foundation in Medical Billing and Medical Coding is not all encompassing. Each of the above examples requires specialty specific knowledge and skills to effectively accomplish Coding and Billing by these areas of specialty, provider type, and services they provide. Inpatient Coding and Outpatient Coding for a hospital are completely different in their guidelines and for a biller, reimbursed in a completely different fashion. It takes additional learning to become proficient in any specialized function. AAPC and AHIMA offer additional certification and credentials for specialized skill sets. These often create more opportunity and increased compensation.

In addition to the healthcare provider environment, there are ample opportunities for these skill sets within insurance carriers. The bills submitted require audit and review to be validated and this is a role for Medical Billers and Medical Coders as well.

5 EMPLOYMENT PROSPECTS

In terms of employment prospects, which is a popular question amongst those exploring Medical Billing and Coding as a career, there are certainly no guarantees that can be made here. It should be reiterated that healthcare is the fourth largest industry in the nation. Healthcare is an essential human need and not a luxury. It is always going to be a leading industry. Perhaps in todays climate, the imminent government reform of healthcare with acts such as The Affordable Care Act and other changes, this may lead to some uncertainty. Well, with an estimated 15% to 20% of the US population without health insurance being a driving force behind such reform, that would only stand to increase the number of insurance claims to be processed if that portion of the population secures health coverage. Additionally, many that have not had health coverage elected not to engage healthcare providers as a financial concern. It is the opinion of this author that healthcare reform will not diminish the demand for qualified professionals in the Medical Billing and Coding Field, it will increase it.

Also mentioned earlier is an epic change scheduled to take place on October 1, 2014 where the system used to represent diagnoses of patients will change. This change is anticipated to create significant opportunity for Medical Coders in particular. This type of change has historically created work backlogs and other similar circumstances. In addition, a certain percentage of the existing coding workforce, especially those nearing retirement have chosen not to learn a new system and therefore there will be attrition further reducing the already inadequate pool of qualified professionals. This will not only provide plentiful opportunity, but it will also serve to increase wages as a function of supply and demand.

It is recommended that if you are exploring this career and favoring it as an option, to commence your training as soon as you are able.

6 FREQUENTLY ASKED QUESTIONS

- **I see so many schools offering Medical Billing and Coding. How do I know which one I should choose?**

    This is certainly a very important decision. There are many reputable organizations that offer a valuable educational experience. Unfortunately, there are some that are inadequate. It would not be ethical to make specific recommendations here. However, there are some things that you should look for including accreditation. However, you should just see the word accredited alone. You should research the accrediting body as well and verify the standing of that organization.

- **The school I am considering said that I would be certified when I complete the course. Will I be?**

    This is unlikely. The exams for AAPC and AHIMA are generally conducted at testing centers contracted by these organizations. The tests are administered under strict supervision and electronically. Do not confuse a Certificate of Completion for a course with a nationally recognized certification. This is a common ploy used by "for profit" education companies to fill their seats. Ask to see something from AAPC or AHIMA showing that you will be certified. Of course, you still need to pass the examination. It is impossible for them to assure you your certification in any case.

- **The school told me that there are only a few seats left and that they may not be able to reserve a place for me if I do not act quickly. However, I am not ready to make a decision under pressure. What should I do?**

    You should not succumb to any pressure. Most of the "for profit" schools use a rolling curriculum. Meaning that students are able to enroll at very regular intervals. Often, new students can join the class each month.

- **The school has offered lifetime job placement assistance. This sounds like a valuable benefit. Does it mean they will always find me a job?**
  Unfortunately, it is a sales tool. They offer to provide assistance. It does not promise employment, or that they will even have leads to provide to you. This often becomes a discouragement only after one has completed a course. Do not base your learning choice on this.

- **The school offers financial assistance. This would be a big help to me. Is this typical?**
  Many programs do offer financial aid. Often through government subsidized programs. Where I have seen students get into a bad position is where a school had them start, telling them that their financial aid was all approved, and it in fact was not. Be sure to be vigilant of your FAFSA status. If you choose to begin a class before you are sure that your loans are in place, you may be doing so at your own risk if there is an obstacle. You may be liable to the school for immediate repayment and may not be allowed to stay enrolled if you are unable to make the payement.

- **The school advertises that their instructors are both experienced and "certified". How do I know?**
  Ask! If the school will not provide the documentation on their instructors, this should be a warning sign. If you have the opportunity, you may ask the instructor directly. You can verify credentials for both AAPC and AHIMA on their web sites.

- **The course is 2 hours a day for 30 days. Is that sufficient to learn the material?**
  NO!! As mentioned in this work, there is a great amount of material to learn and become proficient in. As an instructor in 2 different career schools, our schedules were 3 hours a night, 5 nights a week, for 8 months. That is just under 500 hours. Even that was sufficient only to provide a foundation for the students. Every student is different and has different learning speed and capacities, however less than 500 hours would not be sufficient. 500 hours would be similar to a new employee working for 3 months. That would still be an alarming and amazing rate to be learn all there is to this career.

- **The course is offered on line. Is this as good as a classroom?**
  On line learning today is as common as classroom learning. This depends on the students study habits as well as the manner in

which the class is conducted. For this courses subject matter, it would be advisable to make certain that as much of the on line coursework is interactive with an actual instructor.

- **Should I schedule my certification exam now, or as I near completion of the course?**
  The initial pass rate of the exams is not high. I highly recommend that even the best student gain real world practical experience prior to sitting for the exam. Classroom learning is a very essential element, however it is not a replacement for real world practical experience. The exam covers a number of knowledge categories that really would be best reinforced and understood by being in the environment. In the end, only the examinee can judge their personal readiness and comfort level. Investing in a study guide from the organization that you will be testing with would be a very wise investment and give you the best measure of your readiness.

- **If I don't have my certification, then I can't get a job, and therefore I can't get the practical experience I need. Isn't this a no win situation?**
  Well, let's be honest. Finding a position will be more difficult for someone just starting out. That is true in any industry. However, every person in every job was at one time that person, the one that was starting out with no or little experience. It may take more resumes being sent, it may take more phone calls or interviews, but it is not at all hopeless. Hospitals often have the ability and inclination to take on a certain number of entry level staff. Larger medical practices and even billing services do as well. You may need to start in a different position. Of course, to secure one that has some relationship to your goal position. Ask about pathways to your goal. Highlight your coursework, present yourself competently, confidently, and professionally and you will succeed.

- **I want to work from home. That is why I got into this. I was told this is a way to work form home. Can I?**
  Yes, you can. BUT! Let me offer a few cautions. It is a risk as much as a benefit for an employer to let staff work "remotely". It usually requires a level of confidence in the employee. So, don't be surprised if there is a time period required commuting before you are allowed to do so. The number of coders that work remotely in the industry is very high. However, not all employers are equipped to offer this option and some simply elect not to. If you are basing your work opportunities on this option, it may limit you until you have both the experience and find the opportunity to do so.

- **I saw an ad for a home based business, Medical Billing and Coding From Home. It came with software, claim forms, instructions, and more. It is a lot of money, but I could own my own business. Is this possible?**

  I refer to this as "The Business in a Box". If it was that simple, they would be flying off the shelf at Wal Mart. I could give you a set of wrenches and tell you that you can do auto repair in your garage. That is true, if you know how to repair cars, and people trust you to do it in your garage. The thing that does not come in that box is clients. One key point to consider. The doctor that you are going to solicit to do his or her billing likely has bills to pay just as you do, including those for his or her medical practice. You should have a very good body of experience before even thinking of soliciting a client for that type of service. There are many legal considerations as well as logistical arrangements that must be firmly in place. There are also a large number of established billing services to compete with. Before you take that step, be sure it is one that you are truly prepared for.

- **What kind of salary should I expect?**

  This is a difficult, if not impossible question to answer. There are so many factors including geographic area, budget of the employer, experience, job description, and credential just to name a few. It is a negotiation. There are different ideas of what a successful negotiation is. In this circumstance, it may not be getting what you asked for, but getting what you can live with. It all depends on your needs and objectives and how you are willing to match them to an employers needs and objectives. Start on the higher end and be willing to concede. It is likely the approach an employer will use.

- **I have heard about traveling coders. Do they really exist?**

  They most certainly do. The author of this book has spent nearly a decade traveling to different states working in a number of capacities under contractual coding relationships. There are a significant number of coders that work an almost exclusive travel basis. One must have a body of experience to be considered for these opportunities, usually a minimum of 3 years of experience. However, they do truly exist and can be quite rewarding in many ways including higher pay, paid travel, varied experiences, and more.

7 SUMMARY

The Medical Billing and Coding Field is a great career choice for the right candidates. It offers a wide variety of roles, in a large industry that will not become obsolete. It offers very competitive salaries and fulfilling and challenging career roles. This is a career. It requires dedication, study, accuracy, discipline, and effort. However, it is quite rewarding as well. There are a wide variety of career paths that one can take once in this field. The work of a coder or a biller is important work that has very significant role in many ways. It does require much time and effort to become proficient in, however that effort is rewarded with a satisfying career, competitive salary, and a certain prestige. It may not be for every person. It is the goal of this work to provide the most objective and informative information to aspiring coders and billers so that they can make a very informed career decision. If the information contained in this work influences the reader away from this career decision, it is the hope of the author that it does so in a manner that saves that person a great amount of time and effort that might be lost if not well informed. As mentioned in the Preface, this work comes with unlimited email question support related to this overview and the consideration of this career field. Please feel free to email questions with your purchase ID in the subject line to dbpalmerccsp@yahoo.com

8 RESOURCES

AHIMA -American Health Information Management Association
233 N. Michigan Avenue
21st Floor
Chicago, IL 60601-5809
http://www.ahima.org/
Customer Relations: (800) 335-5535
Main Number: (312) 233-1100
Main Fax: (312) 233-1090

AAPC – American Academy of Professional Coders
2480 South 3850 West, Suite B
Salt Lake City, UT 84120
http://www.aapc.com/
Email: info@aapc.com
Toll Free Phone: 800-626-CODE (2633)
Local Phone: 801-236-2200
Fax: 801-236-2258

AMA - American Medical Association
AMA Plaza
330 N. Wabash Ave.
Chicago, IL 60611-5885
http://www.ama-assn.org
(800) 621-8335

CDC - Centers for Disease Control and Prevention
1600 Clifton Rd.
Atlanta, GA 30333
http://www.cdc.gov/
800-232-4636

HFMA - Healthcare Financial Management Association
Corporate Office
3 Westbrook Corporate Center
Suite 600
Westchester, IL 60154
http://www.hfma.org/
Toll-free: (800) 252-4362
Direct: (708) 531-9600
Fax: (708) 531-0032

NHA - National Healthcareer Association
11161 Overbrook Road
Leawood, Kansas 66211
http://www.nhanow.com
info@nhanow.com

Phone: (800) 499-9092
Fax: (913) 661-6291

WHO – World Health Organization
Avenue Appia 20
1211 Geneva 27
Switzerland
http://www.who.int/en/
Telephone: + 41 22 791 21 11
Facsimile (fax): + 41 22 791 31 11

ABOUT THE AUTHOR

Douglas B. Palmer, BS Health Administration, CCS-P has over 17 years of Practice Management, Revenue Cycle Management, HIM and Consulting experience. He has worked with medical practices of all sizes, been on the management team of some of the countries leading healthcare facilities, and consulted for more leading facilities as well as for leading insurance carriers.

He is expert in all reimbursement methodologies, revenue cycle issues, EMR implementation and HIM management. He has overseen and managed the recovery of millions of dollars in revenue for clients and past employers. As the principal at Phys Assist HIM and Revenue Cycle Consulting, he prides himself on being personally involved and connected with each end every client and exceeding clients expectations as the minimum acceptable outcome.

Mr. Palmer is a specialist in Coder Education as well as Provider Education, and has extensive experience in these areas. His highly successful experience in educating benefits his audiences with his engaging and easy-to-understand approach as well as his style of providing tools, techniques and devices to recall important information.

http://www.audioeducator.com/speakers/douglas-b-palmer

http://managemypractice.com/a-conversation-with-expert-coder-doug-palmer-on-coding-computer-assisted-coding-and-icd-10/

http://www.audioeducator.com/home-health/v-and-e-codes-steer-clear-of-these-common-mistakes-misunderstandings.html

http://www.codinginstitute.com/claim-boosters-bridge-the-gap-between-medical-billing-and-medical-coding.html

www.ingramcontent.com/pod-product-compliance
Lightning Source LLC
Chambersburg PA
CBHW071755200526
45167CB00018B/2202